Tales of an Aspiring Shaman

YVETTE MARKS

ISBN: 978-1-365-78741-6

Photography by Yvette Marks, with the Spirit of Her Own Camera

Cover Design by Scott Gaunt

www.scottgaunt.co.uk

DEDICATION

I was cradled in the trunk of the Llangernyw Yew Tree in the North of Wales, with my beloved drum by my side, when I wrote this dedication:

To my Mother, who gave me so much in Life and who continues to love and guide me from Death;

To my Father, who gave me the fruits of his Life's Labour at just the right time to allow me to go on this adventure in the way that I did;

To my Teachers at the Sacred Trust Teaching Centre for Shamanic Studies, who showed me these most precious of cherished ways; and

To my Allies – my sweet, sweet teachers, my True Teachers.

Thank you and I love you

As my teacher, Simon, so often says, "We do what we do for the children." And so, to the littlies Donovan, Chrysten, Shannon, and Kaylee: my Ancestors are your Ancestors and I dedicate these tales to you.

And to all the littlies out there: the lines of our Ancestors reach back all the way through time, until they find their origin in a single source. So, if you can derive anything that is good and sweet and true out of these stories, then these tales are for you too.

With so much love,
Yvette

28 December 2016

ACKNOWLEDGEMENTS

These stories are about my experiences and my experiences are borne out of everything and everyone I have ever encountered. And so, I want to thank everyone and everything I have ever encountered.

I want to thank that stranger who offered to help me carry my grocery bags. I want to thank the countless people who have given me direction when I was lost. I've had so many teachers in my life and I want to thank them all. I want to thank all the beings who encouraged me not to publish the very first draft of this book the very first minute I'd written it.

When it comes to naming the beings I want to thank, I can see why I need to keep this short.

And so, the people below are named with the intention that they represent all the people I would like to name. And, yes, this is a solution which I have extrapolated from something else I have learned at the Sacred Trust ☺

So, if your name isn't here and, if we have ever crossed paths in any way, you can be certain that I do want to thank you. I have purposefully left out such obviously important names like those of my father, my best friend, awesome lady shamanic teachers and awesome lady supervisors (to suggest but a few.) I'm hoping that this will reassure you, if it is reassurance that you need, that, if your name is not here, then it does not mean that you are not important.

And to the named beings:

Kay Read, for the 8th of August. For what you have been through and for what you have given the world. If you ever write your book, I'll buy it.

Lucien Wood, for inspiring me to get my own camera. I don't just love that photograph you took because it's a beautiful photograph. I love it because it has helped me to remember that our art is sacred.

Mr Patel, I don't know how it is that you fit everything I'm looking for into that tiny shop of yours, but somehow you do. More importantly though, when I hadn't walked for months and was supposed to start trying, it was the thought of seeing a friendly face during the day that gave me the energy to start.

Anette Nilsen, my personal trainer. I wouldn't yet call what I do with you graceful, but it certainly is victorious. You make me laugh while I want to die, and you're helping me to enjoy being in my body again. From my heart, to yours, thank you.

Mr Brewer, you'd had to rush to make that train. I am so glad you did! The more I think of what you told me that day, the more I realise how much it has helped me.

Kathy and Louise Amor, how is it possible to love two people so very much after such a short time? But I do. And I have visited you again and I will visit you again and again and again and again...

Mrs Gwynne, when I next visited Belmont House, I noticed even more pictures on your walls which had me doing double takes. I'm really looking forward to visiting again!

Elina Hytönen-Ng and Kwok Ng, to precious new friendships, Elina, and thank you for introducing me to Kwok. And, Kwok, for reading my book and for checking it. And for encouraging me. And encouraging me. And encouraging me.

Miroslav Ziman, for your friendship, for the happy bees that you keep and for introducing me to them. It remains one of my most treasured memories to this day.

Jerome Salyers, my supervisor. I could not have asked for more. You don't even need to bring out your drum, (although, I have to say, I love it when you do,) I get a healing from you every time we speak.

Simon Buxton, my teacher. What it is to have had someone like you to broker spiritual power on my behalf. What it is to have someone like you to show me how to do this for others. I am so incredibly lucky. And I know it!

Mama: ∞

CONTENTS

INTRODUCTION

PLACES OF GREATEST BLESSING

    PART ONE: YVETTE'S PILGRIMAGE STORY
    PART TWO: STOCKHOLM
    PART THREE: SOMEWHERE IN ENGLAND

THE YEW TREE

WHAT IS GOING ON WITH NAMES?

FLEETWOOD MAC

SPEAKING WITH THE ANIMALS?

THE EARTH AND THE CROWN

MY BODY, MY HOME AND THE LAND

THE TROUBLE WITH INTERPRETATION

SELFISH AND UNSELFISH

DEEPENING INTO THE DREAM

MERCURY RETROGRADE

THE LEGENDS OF THE LAND

WELCOME TO MY WORLD

    PART ONE: THE GRATEFUL DEAD
    PART TWO: AN ANCIENT YEW TREE
    PART THREE: AWAKENING TO THE ROCKS
    PART FOUR: MY FRIEND WHO LECTURES AT OXFORD UNIVERSITY
    PART FIVE: THE PERSON WHO FIRST TOLD ME ABOUT THE SACRED TRUST
    PART SIX: A CYCLONE NAMED YVETTE
    PART SEVEN: UNRAVELLING SOME THINGS THAT HAVE GONE WRONG
    PART ∞: THE BEES

AFTERWORD

ANOTHER AFTERWORD

PS: ∞

AND AN EPILOGUE

INTRODUCTION

Having spent the most wonderful night, dreaming with the Fey, in the most wonderful place, deep in a hidden valley, I went on to spend a wonderful day in places which are surely as magical as the most magical places this world has to offer. My day's end landed on the idea of writing this book.

These stories describe events which are real; events which are as real to me as having my coffee in the morning to whatever it is that I dream about at night. They each have their beginning, their middle or their end (in as much as anything ever really has a beginning, a middle or an end) in something which happened while I was doing my Shamanic Practitioner Training at the Sacred Trust.

As my supervisor on the training reminds me, these threads are still being woven together into a bigger story whose plot and meaning has yet to unfold.

The Shaman and the Madman visit the same place. It's a land of metaphor, where the same thing can be shown to two people in many different ways and where what is shown continues to show more and more over time. The difference between the Shaman and the Madman is that the one goes there on purpose. I have definitely visited these places on purpose and I eagerly look forward to doing so again.

In writing these stories, I have asked for and I have been granted the blessing of my Allies.

It is my hope that, at the very least, whatever time you spend in reading these stories will be a time which you will feel was well spent. I would be honoured if, in any way, anything you read here enriches your life or the lives of those around you. And, if you are interested in exploring the healing you can find in these shamanic ways, it is my heartfelt hope that you will do so.

And, now, on to the stories...

PLACES OF GREATEST BLESSING

One day, Simon taught Yvette a way in which she could connect with the Sun and ask it to show to her a place of Greatest Blessing. Simon also taught Yvette how to ask the Sun to show her a symbol. Yvette would be able to know that she had found the place that the Sun had shown her if she also found the symbol when she actually visited the place.

The three stories that follow speak of what happened when Yvette followed the beams of the Sun to a place of Greatest Blessing. It seems that, like the bee who also follows the Sun, she's hopped from flower to flower along the way. But there's no doubt in her mind that Spirit has always arrived when needed and turned her to face the direction in which she next needed to go.

PART ONE: YVETTE'S PILGRIMAGE STORY

Maria Hendrike van der Merwe bore three children. Her husband, Siegfried, named two of their children and Maria, or Riekie as she was called, named her middle child Yvette. Yvette was not happy when she found out her name didn't mean what she'd always been told it meant. She found out her name meant a Yew Tree or an Archer, which didn't mean anything to her at all.

Time passed and Yvette moved hemispheres and Riekie took up residence in the Land of the Dead. More time passed and Yvette eventually found her way to an amazing, life changing school called the Sacred Trust. It was around that time that she easily came across articles on the internet which just hadn't been there when she had looked before. These articles spoke of the meaning of the yew tree and she began to truly love the name that her mother had given to her.

Set on the task of going on a pilgrimage, she was shown she was to go to a place near a road she had been on before. It ran from Herefordshire into Wales. Once there, she was to find some tin cans of, what she thought to be, Iron Bru littered on the road.

Hansel and Gretel like, Spirit created a trail of clues that led her ever deeper toward her pilgrimage. These clues were so many and so magical, that they are worthy of stories of their own. Most of all though, Spirit spoke to Yvette in a language which had to do with the meaning of names.

It was on a Middle World journey that she came upon an old man drinking from a can that looked exactly like the one she had seen in her sunbeam journey. Looking closer, she saw it was Strongbow Cider which she later learned is brewed in Hereford, which is right near the road she had been shown in her journey. It all just felt so right when she saw the archer on the can and thought of the Archer of her name.

On the date she had carefully chosen, she left her home, carrying two bags and a drum, with her Allies strongly by her side. She walked through the woods, calling on the Spirits of the Land to support her as she did so.

When she arrived at Paddington Station, she felt elated for she had already come across her symbol advertised on a platform. She'd never seen Strongbow Cider advertised in that way before. Up in the sky, it showed a man who looked like a God made up of clouds. He was pointing his arrow at the green land and the apple trees below.

The train to Hereford quickly filled. A peculiar looking man plopped down beside her. A lady walked into the carriage, called out Simon – which told Yvette to listen – and walked straight out again. The man then told Yvette he had just returned from a cycling trip in Germany, which is where Yvette's father now lives and what Yvette's father regularly does.

The man went on to entertain Yvette with the best stories for the rest of the three and a half hour train ride. Some felt like important lessons to her, some reassured her of her own opinions, and some were just plain interesting. At the end of the journey, Yvette smiled to herself as she learned his surname is Brewer and she wondered how she had ever thought he looked peculiar. She was also amused at the thought of an Oxford University trained Maths teacher and an aspiring Shaman travelling together.

Once in Hereford, Yvette and her taxi driver drove back and forth, looking for the farm where Yvette had arranged to stay. They asked a man, tending to a horse at some stables for directions. While the man went into the house to ask if they knew where this farm was, Yvette looked at the horses and wished and wished she could stay with them for longer. Both Yvette and the taxi driver were so shocked when the man returned, saying that, actually, this was the place where Yvette was to stay.

Yvette was very interested when she learned that Kathy, who owned the farm, was Taurus, which is the sign most closely associated with nature. She had suspected that her task on this pilgrimage would involve working with nature and the land, even extending to her own homeland of South Africa.

Left alone to explore, Yvette went outside with her drum. She came upon some horses where she stopped and said the lines, "I close my eyes to see, I stop in anticipation of moving forward and I drop to my heart." As she felt her heart swelling with warmth, two of the horses moved to stand together in a way which made them look like a single heart. She went on to find a field with cows where she drummed for ages while the cows looked on with seeming interest.

She then went into the woods where a Spirit of the Land appeared to her. The Spirit told her the land was soaked in blood and asked Yvette to please help them. She promised to return the next day.

Back in her room that evening, she reflected on how many times the world wars had come up during the day. There were memorials at train stations, stories told by Mr Brewer and the volumes of war poems she had seen lying on Kathy's stove top. She also thought about how Mr Brewer, the taxi driver and Kathy had each talked of travelling to many lands. As she looked at the blue and white striped bed linen in her room, she thought of the many people she'd seen wearing these same stripes throughout the day.

Before she went to bed, her body protector on the alert, Yvette moved her awareness around the house. On the third floor, she found a lady who was folded in on herself just sobbing and sobbing. Yvette tried to get her attention but the lady was just too submerged within her own world of tears. Eventually, one of Yvette's psychopomp Allies descended, larger than Yvette had ever seen her before. Her Ally gathered this sobbing lady in her arms and took her to the Upper World.

On the rainy Monday morning, Yvette called in Spirit and journeyed to receive her task for the day. It was to go back into the woods and do some work on the land. She joked that getting her drum wet was against her moral compass, yet her Ally insisted she go. Dressed and ready, the rain had stopped. At the entrance to the woods, Yvette spent ages calling in all her Allies and the Spirits of everything and everyone she could think of.

The rain returned as though telling her to just get on with it. There in the woods, standing between the Oak and the Holly trees, she drummed for over an hour as, layer by layer, her Allies cleared the land and spoke with the local spirits. Once they were finished, a horde of souls rose up into the sky and set off for the Upper World. Yvette could see they were soldiers and instinctively told them they need no longer march. These soldiers turned to Yvette, raised their caps and, with joyful smiles, they went on their way. Later that afternoon, as Yvette walked the couple of miles into Hereford, she saw a sign which said, "Welcome to Hereford, the city of the Marches."

Back at the farm, Yvette journeyed to receive her next task and she was shown that she was to let Kathy know that she was available for healing. At the very moment Yvette's journey ended, Kathy returned home with her daughter who, Yvette learned, was also Taurus. Yvette very awkwardly told them she could do healing, if wanted. Strangely, when she went into the bathroom afterwards, the light was so much brighter than it had been before.

On Tuesday morning, Yvette noticed there were many volumes of love poems on the breakfast table. Spirit told her that today she was to sit outside and be still. She went back to the field of cows where she said the lines about dropping into the heart again. Every time she felt her heart swelling with warmth, the cows stepped forward and every time she stopped, the cows stopped. This continued, stop-start, stop-start until, eventually, the cows reached the fence and she could stroke them.

She went on to spend a lovely morning outside, being amused by the geese and watching spiders spin their webs while all types of bird flew about overhead. A Spirit of the Land appeared to her and she felt it come and sit with her for a while.

She went to Belmont Abbey for lunch where she journeyed on where she was to stay the following evening. She was told to go to Hay-on-Wye. She came across the most picturesque looking little Bed & Breakfasts on the internet as well as one less picturesque looking one called Belmont House. She suspected that, given she was at Belmont Abbey, Belmont House was to be her destination and, true enough, it was the only place with vacancies.

Back at the farm, Kathy's daughter suggested that her mother might actually benefit from some healing and, when Yvette told her she would be so happy to do it, her daughter asked if she could have some too. It was a beautiful healing and, as her daughter shared her email address, Yvette was touched to learn that their surname means love.

Kathy arrived home and offered to take Yvette out to see the river Wye. As they set off, Kathy told Yvette she had never had any spiritual experiences before. By the end of the walk she had confided that she often saw spots of colour which take on living shape which is exactly what Yvette saw as a little child. While on the walk, Kathy also taught Yvette many interesting facts about nature and how to tell if the land is out of balance.

While eating dinner in the garden, Kathy's daughter mentioned her boyfriend had regularly heard crying on the third floor. Without thinking, Yvette told them she'd seen such a lady who had now gone somewhere nice. Kathy became tearful, saying she had always felt for this lady who she believed had been a Mrs Taylor who had lived in this house before. Mrs Taylor had lost her husband when he and his two brothers had drowned in the river Wye. Writing on her nearby tombstone apparently included lines such as 'Three years a wife and forty seven years a widow' and 'If goodness had the power to save, they would not have gone to their watery grave.'

After dinner, Kathy and Yvette went out back for Kathy's healing. At the end, Kathy took Yvette's drum and the gentle beats she sounded seemed like the rhythm of a heartbeat. They sat out there for ages, eventually settling into silence as the stars came out one by one. Over the woods, where Yvette's Allies had done the land work, the clouds looked like a man holding his hands over the woods as though still giving healing. In the distance, an owl hooted, a horse galloped and a flock of wild geese cried out as they flew in their V shape overhead.

Afterwards, back in the house and chatting, there was a larger than life atmosphere of joy.

On Wednesday morning, Yvette walked around the land to say her goodbyes. At one point, Spirit told her to look up and she asked, "What do you mean, look up?" looking up into the sky as she did so. There, circling silently overhead, was a large bird of prey which reminded Yvette of one of her Allies.

Feeling as though every cell in her being was lit up with love for the people and for the land, Yvette was composing an email to Simon in her head, thanking him for this amazing task. Just as she was doing this, a little pony came galloping forward and stopped at the fence as though waiting for her to go and stroke it. She asked the Spirit of the Land if she was to do anything else and it replied, "Yes, promise to visit again," and she gladly did.

Just before she left, she learned that the meaning of Kathy's surname, while sounding like love, actually derived from a word which can be associated with war.

As Yvette took the scenic bus route from the farm to Hay-on-Wye, she looked at the map to see where in the land she was actually going. She noticed this strange little red line that looked like a border. When she arrived at Belmont House, which turned out to be so lovely and just perfect for her, she had to ask the landlady, Mrs Gwynne, the embarrassing question of which country she was in. She felt pleased when she learned she was in Wales and that her pilgrimage would be spanning two countries because this also has to do with the meaning of her name.

That evening, as she sat in the garden, Yvette became increasingly uncomfortable. Just to her right, where England lay, the skies were calm and a lovely clear blue. Overhead, in Wales, where Yvette was, the clouds formed horizontal layers of red and black demonic shapes (although she doesn't believe in demons anymore.) Later that night, she journeyed to receive her task for the next day. She struggled to interpret it but it was clear she was to prepare for war. On checking her phone, she saw that severe weather warnings had been issued and she wondered if the rain would prevent her from getting home.

On Thursday morning, she awoke to three email messages telling her that her email account had been hacked. One came from the person who had first told her of the Sacred Trust. Another came from her supervisor and the third came from her friend who lectures at Oxford University. This reminded Yvette that it had been an aspiring Shaman and an Oxford University trained Maths teacher that had travelled together some days earlier. That it had now been raised a notch with an actual Shaman and an actual Oxford University lecturer made her feel protected in a way but it also gave her the sense that - excuse my language - this shit had just got real.

Despite the weather warnings, the day was clear and Yvette was shown she was to walk along the river Wye. She left Hay-on-Wye by a little street called Bridge which reminded her of her teacher's teacher. Each time she crossed a bridge, she found her brain automatically repeating a little mantra, thanking her teacher's teacher for teaching her teacher what he's teaching her. Just imagine how she felt when she next saw her teacher and he said he was going to read out words just as his teacher had given them to him!

Before she entered the woods, she called to her Allies and felt as though they formed an army behind her. Strangely calm, she stepped forward to face whatever danger was to be met.

At an idyllic little spot where swans floated down the beautiful river Wye, Yvette was moved to stop and drum. Her Allies worked the land and she saw blessings floating down the river from Wales into England. It was then that the association between war and protection occurred to her.

Having walked along the river side and through some pretty fields, she came to realise there was a road just ahead. She journeyed to find out what she was to do and she was told to wait. There, on that path, parallel to the main road, she felt like an actress waiting in the wings. After some time, she checked in again and was told to now step forward. Feeling every bit the lady with her arm resting upon the arm of Spirt and showered in tingles, she stepped forward and onto the road where there, precisely as she had seen it in her sunbeam journey, was the road she recognised and two cans of Strongbow Cider. Overcome with excitement, she bashed out an email to her supervisor on her phone, "Jerome, Jerome, I've found it! Exactly like it was in my journey, I've found it!"

After some time, she continued forward for a few hundred metres where she came upon the beautiful little church of St Meilig. She journeyed to find out what she was to do here and she was shown to just go inside the church. She pressed on the door and it would not budge. Perplexed, as her journey had shown her going in, she tried again and, this time, the door gave way. In that little medieval church in the Welsh countryside, Yvette felt for the first time, as though her animistic shamanic practice could sit easily alongside a belief in a single creator. She took pictures of her drum resting comfortably and rightfully against the ancient Celtic cross and, clear that the work was done, she walked back to Hay-on-Wye.

Later that afternoon, Yvette received a message from a very dear friend of hers who was with his father while on his death bed. Her friend asked her to say a prayer for him. She went back to the river with her drum where she received the most indescribably beautiful visions of this man's passing.

On Friday morning, Yvette woke to an email from her friend, telling her that this had happened.

As she left Belmont House, she saw a painting of the river Wye on the wall with porcelain wild geese arranged in a V around it. It reminded her of the geese at Kathy's and of films where they animate pictures of the scene at the end of each scene. She felt very much like a character she liked in a story that she liked.

Just as she alighted the bus outside her home in London, she saw another lady wearing those blue and white stripes she'd seen so many people wearing at the beginning of her pilgrimage. It was just about time for the New Moon in Leo and she thought about what the Sign of the Lion has to teach her about the heart.

So many other events and synchronicities took place which will have to wait for another day. The impact and meaning of her pilgrimage is still bursting forth in all directions - backwards, forwards, up, down and spiralling through time.

Strongbow Cider brings Venus and Mars together in that the arrow is a symbol of Mars and the apple is a symbol of Venus.

At the time of Yvette's pilgrimage, Venus and Mars were also travelling together through the sign of Leo. The only time she had ever been on the road she'd been shown in her sunbeam journey was over ten years before, while she had been on holiday in a town called Leominster. If you say it how it's spelled, it's Leo minster or Church of Leo, Church of the Heart.

Yvette has since asked, "Who or what does sharing the part of her story to do with her friend's father's death serve?" The journey she had in response brought a happy photograph from Yvette's childhood album to life. Her journey started with a delighted little

Yvette sitting at the top of a slide in a park while her mother, smiling from ear to ear and with arms wide open, was waiting at the bottom to catch her. They went on to spend a nice time together in the park.

Yvette did not plan for her pilgrimage to last for six days, but somehow her mind has since repeatedly been turning towards the seven days of a creation story. When she went to take the photograph from her album to place it on the altar at the Sacred Trust, she was very nearly overwhelmed when she read the date on the reverse - it was the same date as the seventh day of her pilgrimage - just thirty nine years before!

Now, before she died, Riekie had promised Yvette that, if there was anything on the other side, she would find a way to show her. Until she was twenty, when the meaning of her name suddenly changed, Yvette had been told that her name meant little ruler, which, of course, is Leo.

When she first journeyed on how to tell her story, she helped a horde of souls transcend into the Upper World. In her journey, Spirit came to her clothed in the form of Simon. Referring to the horde, which seemed infinite, she asked him when will this all stop. 'Simon' told her, it never stops, you just have to pick your moment. And so, with a clear and heartfelt commitment that her adventure with Spirit has most definitely not yet stopped, she's going to pick this moment, to say…

The End

PART TWO: STOCKHOLM

Yvette's very first journey to find a place of Greatest Blessing took her to a landscape of a city which had granite rocks and some pastel coloured buildings. Once there, she was shown she was to find a golden covered chocolate coin. When she returned from her journey, she had no idea where this place might be.

When she considered the charming city of Cork, she thought, "Hmm, maybe, but, no." When she considered the gorgeous little Cornish town of Looe, she thought, "Hmm, maybe, but, no." More than two years passed before Yvette was given a reason to think about this sunbeam journey again.

A digression: Yvette has this friend and the way in which Yvette met this friend is one of her favourite of all stories to do with the meeting of friends. Yvette was on the tube, in London, when she committed a bit of a social error. She leaned over her neighbour's shoulder to read her neighbour's book. What's more, when the book took her fancy, Yvette asked her neighbour if she could see the title page. This isn't really commonly acceptable "London Tube Behaviour." Strangely enough, her neighbour was open and friendly and when they realised they were both getting off at the same tube stop, Yvette's neighbour invited her to go for a drink. They've been friends ever since.

One day, this friend told Yvette that she had met a man from Sweden. They soon fell in love and Yvette's friend moved out to Sweden to marry this man. Yvette went to Stockholm to attend her friend's wedding and, in the midst of the wedding excitement and of meeting new people, she was able to explore some of this beautiful city.

The first thing that struck her about Stockholm was how unusual it was compared to the other European cities she'd visited before. Most cities she'd visited had grown around a river and Yvette was used to very quickly finding her way around a new city by orienting herself to the river.

Not so in Stockholm. The city is made up of fourteen islands. It has almost sixty bridges and its centre is situated almost entirely on water. It took a while for Yvette to work out North from South and how to get from A to B. But, oh, it was pretty!

She was on a bus, touring the city, when the recorded voice of the guide started to speak about a fire that had burned down the ancient Tre Kronor castle in the 1600s. A strange kind of 'pay attention' feeling arose within her.

She thought to herself, "Why would this date, the 7th May, when the fire took place, be so important to her?" It was close but not quite the same date as the birthday of someone important to her. She felt caught in a feeling that something of great significance was happening when, suddenly, the granite rocks and the coloured buildings around her made themselves felt. She thought to herself, "Hmm, maybe, most definitely, yes!"

In the days that followed, Yvette was able to see more of this city. At the Vasa Museum, she learned of the great warship which had sank within 1,300 metres of having set sail on her maiden voyage. Themes of her pilgrimage echoed faintly around her head as she learned that the King who had commissioned this warship was also known as the Lion of the North or as the Lion of Midnight. Mars and Venus seemed to be dancing in the background of this story too in that the warship is of Mars and the name of the Vasa's sister ship, the Apple, is a symbol of Venus.

"What was going on with apples?" Yvette wondered. Memories of a weekend training course she had attended at the Sacred Trust before she started her Shamanic Practitioner Training arose. On that weekend, the students had been tasked with journeying for a few words to bring back to the group. The words Yvette had been given by Spirit, which had held such little meaning for her and which she had felt so embarrassed to share, had been that there were plenty of apples for Yvette here and her Allies had told her not to forget her apples. She didn't find the apple an easy symbol to understand. When she looked into it, it sometimes represented the fall of man and sometimes represented his salvation. Like a gun, its meaning seems to depend on the hand who is holding it.

Exploring the city further, she was most impressed with the museums and, in particular, with the number of skeletons she saw on display. Death seemed such a visible part of life here and the human stories told from all those many thousands of years ago made her feel as if the humans of yesteryear were not all that much different to the humans of today.

It was under the city's oldest stone bridge where Yvette found the entrance to the Museum of Medieval Stockholm. As she walked into the little souvenir shop, she noticed a bowl of silver coins next to the till. She thought longingly, "Imagine if those coins were golden covered chocolate coins. I would have found my symbol." Glancing slightly to the right of that bowl and staring at the space as though she were conjuring it out of nowhere herself, there appeared a bowl filled to the brim with golden covered chocolate coins. Can you imagine how she felt when she later learned that the name of the island she was on, Helgeandsholmen, translates into the House of the Holy Spirit?!

The exact nature of the Greatest Blessing that Stockholm has to offer to Yvette is yet to be revealed.

A yoga teacher whose teaching Yvette so loved has now moved back out to Sweden. She gave birth to her first child, a baby girl, within weeks of Yvette's friend from the tube giving birth to her first child, a baby boy. Yvette has met a wonderful Shaman from Stockholm who has shared with her some of the magic to be found in the hidden wisdom of the Runes.

And then, there's the wedding of Yvette's friend. Memories of that wedding still warm her heart to this day. The wedding party was small and intimate and coloured with such joy. Everyone seemed united in such a strong flow of support for the couple. The love between the newlyweds was palpable.

The speeches were lovely. It was particularly the words of the best man which Yvette remembers, of the man being an upward pointing triangle and the woman being a downward pointing triangle. "When these triangles come together," he said, "They form a star to remind us from where we come."

And of all that moved Yvette, what moved her most was the fact that, in getting married, her friend, whose name holds the meaning of a bee, had her surname changed from sand into a flower. And the type of flower her friend can find in her new surname is the type which some people refer to as the Queen of Flowers.

Yvette already has another visit to Stockholm planned to see her friend again and to learn more from her teacher of the Runes. Who knows what blessings are yet to unfold…

(P.S. The words about the triangles and the stars is not a political statement on sexuality. Yvette has never understood why we define each other by our sexuality. Surely, as long as it's consensual and between adults, who people sleep with isn't anyone's business other than the people being slept with? She just found the image these words evoked to be beautiful.)

PART THREE: SOMEWHERE IN ENGLAND

This story begins with Yvette's mother who had died some years before this story starts (if, indeed, it is here that the story starts.)

Yvette had been on the Shamanic Practitioner Training for around five months when she went on holiday to the South of France. She was wandering around the house she was staying in, completely absorbed with whatever it was that she happened to be thinking about when, suddenly, she jumped back in fright. Right in the middle of her head, in her mind's eye - not as a thought, not as a vision - but intensely real and for only an intensely split second, her long since deceased mother had appeared, saying, "Boo!"

Boo. Just as she might have said when Yvette was a child. The entire family would regularly hide behind doors and jump out to give whoever next came by a fright, and then collapse in laughter when they succeeded.

Yvette felt a bit shaken by what had happened but there was no lingering sense of unease or of fear and so she carried on with her holiday. Five months later, Yvette was back at the Sacred Trust again, on another training component. They were learning about the shamanic views on death and dying and what it is that the Shaman can do to help the deceased.

Set on the task of going out into the world to see who might need help, Yvette followed her mind's eye to the home of her teenage years, the very place where her mother had stepped from this world into the next. She really didn't know why she was going there as she really didn't expect to find anything but, sure enough, there her mother was. When Yvette asked her mother what she was doing there, her mother replied that she had known that Yvette would come to look.

Her mother went on to tell Yvette that she did indeed need help to get to where she needed to go. Although Yvette wasn't entirely convinced that her mother really needed her help, her mother continued that she would not be going anywhere until Yvette made her a promise. Yvette had to promise her mother that she would make friends with a certain person. Half Yvette's mind seemed suspended somewhere in ice - stunned with the disbelief that, here she was, reunited with the mother she had mourned so desperately, and, instead of joyfully reuniting, they were arguing. The other half of Yvette's mind was fully involved in doing whatever it would take to win that argument.

Yvette lost the argument. She handed over the promise her mother had asked for and her mother went, somewhat smugly, thought Yvette (smiling at the memory) on her way.

A few months later, Yvette was lying in the dark, communing with the Spirit of Darkness, when her mother suddenly appeared again. This time, she seemed angry. "You've not done what I asked for!" "Ok," replied Yvette. "No, I haven't. You tell me how to do it." Her mother was silent. "Fine," said Yvette, "If you don't even know how to do it, just give me some more time." Her mother vanished.

Two events then happened at almost the same time. Firstly, Yvette was told that the person her mother had wanted her to make friends with was, suddenly and unexpectedly, moving from abroad to England. Secondly, Yvette journeyed to the Sun to find out where in England would hold the greatest blessings for the astrology workshops she was planning on running.

In the months that followed, Yvette located the exact town she had been shown in her sunbeam journey. She found a shop that would be perfect for her workshops. The image on the home page of the shop's website was even of the statue that could be found in the garden at the Sacred Trust.

Yvette arranged workshop after workshop but no matter how high or how low these workshops were priced, no one came. Well, one person came once! Without a doubt, she knew her ideas were good and she knew she was more than qualified to deliver them. It made no sense whatsoever that no one was coming.

One day, Yvette's father came to visit her in London. He told her where the person Yvette's mother had wanted her to make friends with now lived. Yvette could not believe it. Out of all the places in all of England, this person had moved to the exact same town Yvette had been shown in her sunbeam journey.

Yvette's father arranged a meeting between Yvette and this person and, on the same day that this meeting took place, Yvette held her first workshop which was attended by a decent number of people. Yvette and this person did chat a while. They've not really made friends though.

Her mother has since told Yvette to write down everything it was that this person did to upset her so much. Her mother then told Yvette to send it to this person. Her mother told Yvette that she's not doing this for anyone's benefit other than Yvette's own. In sending the letter, Yvette has released all the opinions and all the grudges she's held for so long and she's not yet filled the space with anything new.

She's extrapolating from something that Simon once said on the Spirit of the Drum workshop when he'd been teaching the group to drum as one mind. The group had managed to establish a rhythm which everyone was holding in place when he said, "It's alive, let it change." And it feels good.

THE YEW TREE

Early on in the Shamanic Practitioner Training, Yvette realised it would be nice to increase her knowledge around nature. And so, she ordered a set of oracle cards to do with the trees.

On the day the cards arrived, Yvette excitedly shuffled them with the intention of selecting one card which would tell her more about her role in life. How exciting: her first answer to the first question she had asked was the Yew Tree, the meaning of her name. As she looked at the cards, she began to realise that, although they were going to be a wonderful addition to her collection of tarot and oracle cards, they just weren't going to teach her much about the trees.

A few hours later, a friend of hers arrived to visit. Yvette's friend wanted to do some remote healing work on a client of hers and would need to go out into the woods to find something of nature to represent her client. Yvette decided to accompany her. As they were getting ready to leave, one of Yvette's Allies caught her attention and he told her that he was going to show her something "Really Good."

How very exciting! Yvette started dreaming of learning to translate the song of the birds or to track animals by the markings they made in the earth. As Yvette and her friend approached the entrance to the woods, Yvette's eye was drawn to the notice board. It's a board she passes almost every day, but, because someone had just pinned something to it, and, because the sun reflected brightly off the glass cover as it was being closed, Yvette couldn't help but notice it and go look.

The announcement on the noticeboard said that, on the very next day, there was to be a free tree identification walk. "Is this what you mean by what you're going to show me?" Yvette asked her Ally. Her Ally burst out laughing, nodding 'Yes,' and Yvette felt the mirth rising up within her in response. Ok - no singing to the birds then - just an ordinary tree identification walk. But it was something she had wanted to learn.

On the next day, Yvette met the group for the tree identification walk and she spent a lovely morning being shown how to identify the trees of the woodland where she lived. She could barely contain her delight when she found out that, right beneath her window, where she had been living for seven years, and unknown to her for all that time, there was a Yew Tree!

WHAT IS GOING ON WITH NAMES?

If you have read Yvette's pilgrimage story, you will know that, at one time in her life, the meaning of her name suddenly changed. Well, that's not all there is to it.

When she first discovered that her name didn't mean what she had always been told it meant, she felt as though her identity had, in some fundamental way, been changed.

At the time, Yvette told her best friend what had happened to her name, and her friend replied, saying that, actually, her own name held a meaning very similar to the one that Yvette had just lost. So, not only had Yvette just lost the meaning of her own name, her best friend had, in Yvette's mind, just acquired it. Yvette has since gone on to love the new meaning of her name but unusual things to do with names continue to happen.

The only time Yvette had ever been to the road she was shown in her sunbeam journey for her pilgrimage was over ten years before when she had been on holiday in Leominster. At that time, she had been there with three friends. Just before Yvette went on her pilgrimage, she attended the Sacred Trust's Spirits of Nature workshop as she'd felt that her pilgrimage would have to do with nature and the land. She met so many lovely people on that workshop, but, out of all the lovely people she met, there have been three people with whom she has kept in touch.

These three people seem to link, by their names or by the meanings of their names, to both Yvette's pilgrimage and to her holiday in Leominster over ten years before.

The first person is called Kathy and Yvette stayed with a Kathy on her pilgrimage. The second person's name means rock and, when Yvette was on holiday in Leominster, she was there with someone whose name means rock. The third person's name means a traveller, a protector against fire and a patron of stones. This not only links to the other two people who have names that have to do with rocks (stones) but also to another person who was on that holiday in Leominster who has a name which means borne of fire.

It was this man whose name means 'borne of fire' who gave Yvette a copy of the book "the Celestine Prophecy." It was the second and only other time Yvette has owned a copy of this book. Her first copy had been given to her by someone else with the exact same name, around four years prior to this.

These two messengers from the Fire have seemingly popped into her life, given her the book and popped right out again. It reminds Yvette that the very first person to ever teach Yvette that the 'magic is real' also has a surname which comes of the fire.

It was towards the end of her Shamanic Practitioner Training when Yvette's father came to visit her in London. They had such a special time together, really bonding in a way that they hadn't had the opportunity to do in years. Before he left, Yvette asked him if he had any of his ancestor's birthdates. She wanted to plot as many of her ancestors' birth charts as possible. Her father replied saying that, actually, he had just started to build up their family tree. He promised to share it with Yvette when he got home. Without knowing why she did so, for it seemed obvious that she knew the names of her grandparents, Yvette went on to check the name of her father's mother and the name of her father's father. "Yes, you're right," he replied, "Those are their names."

But when her father sent Yvette the family tree he had started on, Yvette had to phone him, in confusion. "But, who are these people?" she asked. Her father pointed out one strange name as being her grandmother and another strange name as being her grandfather. "I don't understand," Yvette said. "I even checked their names with you before you left?" Her father just laughed and replied, saying, "Yes, they were called by the names that you know, but these are their real first names."

It seemed to Yvette as though the alchemy of Yvette and her father's bonding, and of what her father had done while in the UK, had resulted in some form of healing of the family. It seemed to Yvette that this healing had even washed backwards into the family line, to the extent of visibly changing the names by which Yvette knew her grandparents.

When a friend of Yvette's came to visit and Yvette shared this story with her, Yvette found that her friend had a story of her own.

Adopted as a baby, the same surnames that could be found in her birth family half way across the world could also be found in her adoptive family.

It seems we're all in this together!

FLEETWOOD MAC

Over a period of days, Yvette became more and more obsessed with some of the songs of Fleetwood Mac. In particular, it was a live performance of Rhiannon which called to Yvette to play the song over and over again. Who knows if it was Yvette, Fleetwood Mac or life itself that was dressed up for a date with Mystery, but a number of things began to happen at the same time.

With her obsession showing no signs of abating, Yvette started to read more about the band. First she read a book about Stevie Nicks. Then she read Mick Fleetwood's autobiography.

She thought about their success and she thought about their powerful music. She thought about their drive and their commitment to "play on" in spite of the numerous challenges and the fraught relationships they faced. Yvette felt inspired. She thought to herself, "What is it that we cannot do, if only we would all work to a common goal?"

The more she read, the more she thought how closely Fleetwood Mac's creativity looked like some of the shamanic ways she was being taught. There was Stevie Nicks' reported interest in all things esoteric. There was the way in which she seems to have almost channelled some of her lyrics. There was Mick Fleetwood's self-reported passionate plea to the powers that be. There was the way he then went on to do whatever he could do to make his vision of himself in a band come true. Mick Fleetwood's famous wooden balls seemed, to Yvette, to be very much like a power object. The lyrics to their song 'The Chain,' a song which is credited to every single member in the band, 'And if you don't love me now, you will never love me again, I can still hear you saying, you would never break the chain' seemed, to

Yvette, to be both full of wisdom and a magically powerful spell.

When Yvette read of Mick Fleetwood drumming in a way which is opposite to the way in which most drummers drum, she thought, "Here's something I can relate to." The more she read, the more she could see ways in which she, herself could relate with them. The way in which Stevie Nicks' work ethic was described, sounded so very much like the way in which she saw her own. Stevie Nicks' Sun in Gemini and Moon in Capricorn seemed to mirror Yvette's own Sun in Capricorn and her own Moon in Gemini.

She saw a yew tree connection linking Mick Fleetwood's name with her own, in that one of Mick Fleetwood's family names is Kells. At around the same time that she had learned this, she had also found out that there is an illuminated manuscript called the Book of Kells. As one theory goes, this manuscript may have originated on Iona, an island whose name originally meant something like Yew place.

And still, that song, Rhiannon, called to Yvette to be played over and over again. Lines of the song stood out from the rest; first one and then another. The line, 'She's like a cat in the dark and then she is the darkness' reminded Yvette that when she had been immersed in the Darkness at the Sacred Trust, cats had almost constantly played against the back of her eyelids. The line, 'Takes to the sky like a bird in flight' reminded Yvette of a Deity of the Sky she so loves to work with. Almost every time Yvette went to draw a Goddess Oracle card, it was Rhiannon which landed in her hand.

One day, Yvette was at home, immersed in Darkness, when suddenly she started speaking automatically. She listened to her own voice telling her more about her own astrology chart. The words gave her new insights into Yvette's Mercury which has to do with the mind, and into Yvette's Neptune which has to do with dreams. After some time, it seemed to her, that an intense and deep understanding of the lines at the end of the song Rhiannon, 'Dreams unwind, love is a state of mind' opened before her.

She felt she had experienced the briefest of moments of what it might be like to engage with the world, with the universe even, as though she were in love with the all of it.

SPEAKING WITH THE ANIMALS?

One day, the students at the Sacred Trust were sent out onto the land with the intention of having an adventure. Yvette's first stop was at the fields with the horses where she spent some time patting the large black stallion. She said to the stallion, with regret, "I'm so sorry, we're not allowed to feed you."

The horse, slowly and purposefully, or so it seemed, turned around and, bum facing Yvette, he dropped a large poo to the ground. Slowly - almost insolently - he turned around, lowered his nose to his poo, sniffed at it and took one step forward so that, again, he was face to face with Yvette, looking her straight in the eye. That expression in his eye, surely she was not imagining it? It was filled with intelligence as though the horse had understood her and was now telling her what he thought of it. Could this horse actually be telling Yvette that she was talking shit?!

Knowing her intention was to have an adventure, she left the horse and continued on her walk around the land. She'd been in the woods for quite some time when she felt a growing sense of unease. She wasn't quite sure how to get out of the woods and she was worried she was going to be late back for class.

Just as her unease began to grow into alarm, a little forest animal - not quite a mouse, not quite a squirrel and not quite a bunny - dashed out from the left. Straight as an arrow, it sped straight down the path. Yvette followed it for a bit until it darted purposefully to the right, into the thick of the woods. Yvette followed it off the path and, not even a couple of metres later, she came out onto open land and she knew where she was. Had this strange little creature of the forest actually responded to her need for direction?

About six months later, she was back at the Sacred Trust for a weekend component when every single time she went out onto the land she saw those shy and gentle creatures she so loved to see, the deer. She'd often seen the deer before, but not like this, not every single time she went out onto the land. What's more, this time, these creatures just did not seem shy.

One early morning, Yvette walked past the deer and, instead of leaping away into the hedges as they usually did, they stayed exactly where they were, peacefully grazing. Yvette went to sit at the foot of the ancient Oak tree and the grazing deer just continued to graze, looking up at Yvette from time to time.

One midday, she was walking along a path when she felt moved to stop and say the lines, "I close my eyes to see, I stop in anticipation of moving forward and I drop to my heart." As she felt her heart swelling with warmth, from behind the long grass, just a few short metres away, a deer jumped into sight. Yvette and the deer, both still, just gazed upon each other. The gaze lasted for some long moments until it was Yvette who stepped away.

In the evening, just as the sun was going down, Yvette walked out onto the land. There was a little deer grazing. As it began to bounce away, Yvette thought, "Oh, please don't go." At that very moment, the little deer stopped, turned to Yvette and looked at her. It moved calmly to the hedge, stopping to look at Yvette every now and again. That little deer stayed out on that field, in full view, for quite some time while Yvette just looked on in amazement.

There was one point on that weekend when Yvette had been tasked with making something. She then buried it overnight in the ground. The next morning, just after she retrieved it, two deer came galloping towards her. Not sure who was more shocked by the encounter, Yvette or the deer, the deer veered sharply to one side where they went up a little hill. Instead of running away into the bushes, one little deer ran back and forth along the hedge. Every now and again, it stopped and looked directly at Yvette while she looked on in astonishment.

Some months later, Yvette was on an adventure in Wales when she decided to visit Emrys Myrddin, a privately owned hill associated with the legends of Merlin. She thought she had found the place and she was about to get out of her car when a dog came running purposefully to her car door. With this dog that Yvette didn't know at her door and no dog owner in sight, Yvette didn't want to get out of her car. She drove on a bit further but soon she realised that the only place to get onto that hill was where she had encountered that dog. Returning to the spot, she found that the dog was still sitting in the middle of the road as though it was waiting for her. The dog looked at Yvette, right in the eye, as though telling her to get out of the car.

Once out of the car, Yvette spent some time trying to open the farm gate to get on to the hill when she saw the dog was waiting patiently for her at another little gate especially designed for the people on foot. As she went to this gate, the dog made it clear it was going to go with her. From the moment they started up that path, it was obvious that the dog knew the way. The dog led her to the top of the hill, waiting for her at gates and at forks in the path. Strangely, it didn't once respond to her voice and it didn't once allow her to pat it.

Having spent some time at the top of the hill, she started to look for the path back down. She could easily see the farm house at the bottom but she just could not seem to find the path. The dog appeared out of nowhere. It started sniffing along the edges of the plants which formed a circle around the hilltop. Yvette thought to herself, "What a good system of finding the path again." "But," she continued to herself, "I could very easily twist my ankle on this uneven ground." The very second she had this thought, the dog raised its head and moved very quickly in a straight and purposeful line, diagonally across the hilltop and directly to the path which took Yvette back down to where she needed to go.

She's since journeyed a number of times to ask about these experiences with animals. Most of these journeys begin with a Deity Yvette loves to work with breathing into Yvette, giving her stars and telling her she is loved.

Now, sometimes (ok, most times,) when Yvette journeys, she is so interested in understanding what the journey might mean, that she finds it difficult to avoid interpreting it before the journey has ended. Given her Allies work outside of Time and Space, Yvette overcomes this difficulty of hers by writing down a number of journey intentions on a number of pieces of paper. Blindfolded, she then picks up a piece of paper and journeys for the answer to the intention on the piece of paper she has just selected. In this way, she can allow the journey to unfold without trying to understand or direct it. She tends to use this method for most of her journeys.

When she journeyed to ask, "What do all these experiences with the animals mean?" for the purposes of writing this story, her journey began with the Deity giving Yvette a rose and squeezing her shoulder. Yvette went into the woods, twirling the rose like a baton, and a little baby bee landed on her finger. She carried it carefully on her finger through to the tree she always goes up. When she got to the tree, she saw an object which she'd once created in a Path of Pollen Ceremony in ordinary reality (as if the reality of a ceremony can ever be called ordinary!) which totemically links her to the hive. She was lifted to the Upper World, where a horse was waiting for her. She rode him side saddle with the little baby bee resting in her lap. Her Ally came forward enthusiastically, excited to see the baby bee. Another Ally smiled so indulgently, Yvette thought, "You could be this baby bee's grandfather." When she met the last Ally on her journey, her Ally touched the bee with affection, gave it a spoonful of honey and the little bee flew happily out the window. Yvette asked this Ally, "What is the answer to my question please?" and her Ally replied, "Look after the bees."

Perhaps it is a reminder to look after the animals in whatever small ways she can. They have personalities, instincts and politics too. There are countless stories of their affection, their courage and of the extraordinary feats they have undertaken on our behalf.

Although she hasn't eaten meat since she was nineteen years old, Yvette genuinely believes that different people have different dietary needs and she would never want to criticise anyone for eating whatever it is that their body needs. She can imagine though, the arrival of an alien from outer space. She can imagine it seeing, for the first time, the ways and conditions in which we, as the entire human race, raise and keep animals for our own use. She can imagine how the alien might see this as the most grotesque of horror films the people of outer space may ever have seen before.

If she had the power to make one plea to which anyone who reads this might listen, it would be to beg of you to consider where your food is coming from and to make any changes that are within your power to make so that you move toward supporting ethical sources.

(P.S. It turned out that the horse was right! Yvette later found out that she could share the green grass on her side of the fence with the animal and she has many a happy memory of having done so since.)

THE EARTH AND THE CROWN

One day, Yvette was at the Sacred Trust when she told Simon that something unusual seemed to be happening quite a lot. Other people would have experiences or would say things in a way which was completely opposite to how Yvette was experiencing or interpreting things. This had even happened with some things that she had experienced with Simon.

As is so often his way, Simon effortlessly made it seem possible that two things which seemed to contradict one another could both be valid and could both exist at the same time. He went on to remind her of the Kabbalists who saw beginnings in endings and endings in beginnings.

Later that weekend, she'd been tasked with creating some sacred art to do with the element Earth. Completely engrossed in what she was doing, she put her piece of paper on top of her drum and began to draw. Her pen accidentally moved off her piece of paper and continued to make markings upon her drum. She felt a bit guilty, thinking that, probably, she shouldn't have been leaning on her drum.

A few weeks later, Yvette had the opportunity to practice some of the techniques she'd been taught that weekend in relation to working with Nature and the Land. As she worked, it began to rain gently and she saw the rain drops bleed into the ink markings on her drum. The ink moved in its entirety, not even leaving the tiniest mark on the original spot, to rest with the manufacturer's branding of the drum, a crown, some distance from its original spot.

It reminded her of the Kabbalistic Tree of Life. The tree of life is a mystical symbol which has been said to explain many things and which has been said to explain everything. One of these things it is said to explain is the process of creation – from its most intangible state within no-thing, becoming ethereal as it moves into existence at the top of the tree, at heaven or at the crown, and taking on more substance as it travels down the tree. Finally, it takes form or manifests at the bottom of the tree, at the Kingdom of Earth.

To her, the markings of the Element Earth had come to represent Earth itself, the tenth sphere on the Tree of Life. To her, the manufacturer's branding of the crown had come to represent Heaven or the Crown, the first sphere on the Tree of Life. And, on her drum, to her, the Earth was now perpetually and visibly joined with the Crown.

She thought about how this had happened. Through rain and through her drum. Through working with intent, with Spirit and with the body of the Land. She thought of rain as the element water which, astrologically, in the form of Neptune and Pisces, can be seen to link us with Spirit. She thought of her drum as the symbol of her beating heart. She thought about how close Spirit can get to us through the waters of our own bodies.

And, she thought, if she allows these waters to move upon her own heart, what is there that cannot be erased, cleansed, shifted or connected with something new?

MY BODY, MY HOME AND THE LAND

Alongside her Shamanic Practitioner Training, Yvette often enjoyed going to a wonderful monthly shamanic group in London where she was introduced to other journeying intentions. In preparation for one such day, she was invited to think about a piece of land nearby her home with which she would like to work. At the same time, within her own journey work, Yvette understood that Spirit was telling her to extend the way she perceived the boundaries of her home to include the woodland behind her building.

At the monthly London group, the attendees were guided to journey to the land they had each chosen to work with. Yvette met with the Spirit of the Land behind her home. It told her that it represented everything that was part of or on that land at any one time, including the plants, the people who visited and even the litter. Yvette understood that whenever she met with this Spirit again, she would be able to tell how the land was doing based on how well the Spirit looked to be to her.

Yvette planned to do more work with this land. On the day she'd planned to do this, she awoke with some unfortunate sensations travelling through her body. She soon realised that this was to be a day when she would be forced to spend some quality time with her toilet. The symptoms were so intense that she fully expected to be house bound for a few days but, not even a few hours later, she felt it was safe enough for her to venture out and do the work on the land, as she had planned.

As she walked towards the place where she'd wanted to work, Yvette started wondering how she would ever be able to tell if any of the work she and her Allies had done would have a lasting impact on the land. She thought that, if the Spirit of the Land represented the land and all that was on it, then, surely, when Yvette and her Allies were there, the Spirit of the Land would look well - but how could Yvette be certain that the Spirit of the Land would still be well once Yvette and her Allies had left?

As Yvette approached a certain hornbeam tree which is especially special to her, she saw an unusual object placed upon one of its trunks. As she drew closer, she realised that someone had left a bag of their dog's poo on this tree, rather than placing it in one of the many bins provided. Yvette didn't really want to clean up after some unknown dog, but she also felt strongly that she didn't want the dog's poo left upon this tree to which she felt so connected.

Having cleared the space - literally - Yvette and her Allies did the work as planned. As she was walking back to her home, the connection between her own symptoms earlier that day and the dog's poo on the tree suddenly occurred to her. Had her question around whether or not anything she did with the land having a lasting impact somehow been answered by her having been shown that there is a very physical connection between her and this tree? "No," she thought to herself, "Surely I'm making this up?"

When she returned to her own flat, she realised that the gutters running alongside her rooftop had been cleared. How could this be? She lived in the top floor flat of a three storey building. Just a few days before, she had noticed how clogged the gutters were and had been meaning to call her landlord to have them cleared. She had been home most of that week and hadn't heard any workers putting up ladders to get to the rooftop to clear the gutters.

Yvette is sure there is an ordinary reality explanation for all this. But she is also clear that this is a very visible reminder of what is true for us all: we are linked to our environment and the well-being of one very much affects the well-being of the other.

THE TROUBLE WITH INTERPRETATION

One magical week while Yvette was staying at one very magical place, she was experiencing synchronicity after synchronicity. One of these had to do with her dreams.

Each night, as she usually did, Yvette went to bed and each night, as she usually did, she dreamed. Each morning, she awoke and, as she usually did, she wrote down what she could recall of her dreams. But, rather unusually, each morning, at breakfast, one of the people she was staying with would start speaking about something that Yvette had just been dreaming of during the night before. It seemed as though the pictures of the night were continuing seamlessly on into the conversation of the day.

One night, as she lay sleeping, Yvette dreamed of a little fox. While the rest of the landscape appeared as it may well do when awake, the little fox took on the form of a cartoon drawing. This baby fox cutely fluttered his eyes and, in a cute little voice, he said, "If you loved me, you would build me a house," and he flicked his eyes to his right. Yvette followed the direction of his eyes where a little house was neatly demonstrated. The fox cutely continued, "And if you really loved me, from time to time, you would let me out." Again, she followed the direction of his eyes back to the house where she saw the roof of the house opening in the way that a lid on a box may well do.

Suddenly, she awoke with the desperate and urgent need to pee. She fumbled her way down the stairs in the dark, through the kitchen, and to the little utility room she needed to get through to get to the toilet.

To her utter frustration, she discovered she couldn't open the door to the utility room. Absolutely desperate and unable to find a light switch, she realised the door had been tied shut. Frantically, she ripped at the tape, the door sprung open and out darted the three little kittens which Yvette now realised had been put to bed in the utility room.

Having relieved herself, Yvette was greeted with the sight of the three little kittens darting here, there and everywhere. They were playing with each other, knocking things over and creating general havoc. Desperately, Yvette would catch one, put it back into the little room and go on to try to catch the next one, only for the first one to come trotting out again.

Eventually, Yvette gave up and returned to bed. It suddenly occurred to her that this event had been uncannily similar to her dream. So, she thought, "What was this? A synchronicity? A prophetic dream? Or were those sweet little kittens capable of reaching into the depths of Yvette's dreams and making her fulfil their wishes?"

She later journeyed to her Allies to find out more. She wrote a number of journey intentions down on a number of pieces of paper. On one of these little pieces of paper, she wrote, "Please tell me more about this dream. Was it a synchronicity, the cats reaching into my dreams or was it a prophetic dream?"

Having journeyed blindfolded on the answers to all the intentions on all the pieces of paper, she listened to the journey she had recorded in response to this intention.

Her journey began with Yvette leaving her body. She left through her front door where she collected a blessing from one of the Deities she works with. This blessing took the form of a substance, similar to the way in which Yvette had read of some mediums being able to manifest an ectoplasm. This substance began to clothe her body. She went into the woods where a Nature Spirit accompanied her to the tree she always goes to. Here, she came across one of her Allies in the form of a tarot lady.

Yvette asked this tarot lady if she would please provide the answer Yvette had come for. The tarot lady shuffled the cards and turned over three cards, one by one. As the tarot lady turned the first card over, Yvette said, "The past card is the Fool." As the tarot lady turned the second card over, Yvette said, "The present card is the Nine of Cups" and, as the tarot lady turned the third card over, Yvette said, "The future card is the Empress."

Yvette had been speaking out loud so she could record her journey and listen to it later. In her journey, she had assumed the three cards would mean past, present and future. Now that she saw the question to which this answer belonged, she thought, "The answer is only giving me three cards to go with three questions. It could be anything then?!"

She thought about it some more. She thought that these cards probably mirrored the option they were matched with. This would put the Fool card with the idea of the dream having been a synchronicity. It would put the Nine of Cups together with the idea of the cats having reached into Yvette's dreams and it would put the Empress card together with the idea of Yvette's dream having been prophetic.

Each of these cards seemed, to Yvette, to be confirming the option with which they were matched.

The Fool card speaks of wholeness. It reminds us that we can tell how one part of the whole is doing by looking at another part. Kind of like synchronicity.

The Nine of Cups speaks of wishes being granted. If those cats had actually reached into Yvette's dreams, their wishes would most certainly have been granted.

The Empress represents all that is feminine. She is able to take that which exists in a potential form, to create it in reality and to then look after and nurture it as it grows.

So what was the answer then? It could be anything? It could be a synchronicity, it could be the cats having reached into her dream and it could also be a prophetic dream.

It's true that her intention was poorly written as it's not easy to interpret the response when there are three questions in the intention. However, Yvette went on to think that the clue she had been given was in the blessing she received from the Deity at the beginning of her journey. The blessing had taken the form of something which manifested from one reality into another and which then clothed her.

It would appear, Yvette thought, that she could, to some extent, create the answer that she wanted.

But somehow, in doing so, she would need to find an answer which allows for growth and depth of understanding without avoiding looking at that which she would rather not see.

SELFISH AND UNSELFISH

One day, Yvette saw a number of people for astrology readings. Two of her clients had such challenging events underway that Yvette offered them some shamanic healing.

On the date that they'd agreed, the first of these two ladies arrived. She started to tell Yvette a story and Yvette began to feel strange. She was certain she'd heard it before but she couldn't remember this lady having ever told it to her. The healing went ahead as planned and the lady left.

A few days later, the second lady arrived. As they began to speak, it became clear that this lady expected Yvette to have remembered a story she'd told her when they'd first met. How strange! Of course Yvette remembered the story. It was almost exactly the same story that the first lady had told her.

Both ladies told stories about their mother's mother having survived one of our world history's most horrible events. But both of these survivors refused to talk about what had happened to them. The one survivor told her grandchild that the only way she had survived was by being selfish. The other survivor told her grandchild that the only way she had survived was by being unselfish.

The lady whose grandmother had survived by being selfish had a number of difficulties. The most obvious one was that she had been painfully and dangerously anorexic. The lady whose grandmother had survived by being unselfish also had a number of difficulties. The most obvious one was that she had suffered from bulimia.

Yvette has since asked, "What is the message I can share about this story?" She put her questions on pieces of paper, blindfolded herself and journeyed for the answer to the question she had just selected.

The journey began with Yvette receiving a flower from a Deity. As she continued along her route, she suddenly started to feel a very real, ordinary reality pain in her back. It felt as though something were poking her from within. Within her journey, Yvette felt as though the place of the pain might be where an angel's wing might grow.

When she met with one of her Allies, Yvette asked if they could help her. They dug around in her back and it became clear Yvette would need an operation. As they operated on her, they pulled out a large tiger which bounded off into the unknown.

As Yvette continued on her journey, the throbbing pains continued but to a lesser extent. Every time she felt a little stab in her back, a tiger kitten leapt out from the hole that the operation had left and ran off into the distance.

When she reached her next Ally, her Ally stitched her up and told her the answer to her question was to do with the birthing of instincts.

The meaning of this journey will have many layers and will unfold over time. At the time of writing, Yvette understands that her story about her two clients is about the instincts we inherit from the way others have handled their challenges. Yvette also understands this to mean that if we have inherited instincts we don't like, we're not necessarily stuck with them. Spirit will help. And the work we do on ourselves is an offering to this world and to all the worlds as new instincts are then created. Yvette's journey seemed to suggest that the work that these two ladies wanted to do on themselves could even be turning them into angels. Their work on themselves has given birth to this story.

When Yvette later journeyed to ask if there was anything else to add to this story, she came across Miss Piggy typing a story. Yvette's Allies were clear, they wanted to throw Miss Piggy out. Yvette understands this to mean that it is time for the author of all our stories to change; there is more than enough for everyone.

When Yvette later emailed this story to these two ladies to check they were ok with Yvette sharing this story, she wanted to send them the exact same email. She emailed the first lady and then copied and pasted it so as to email the second lady. But it pasted with all the text highlighted. She tried this a couple of times before she decided to copy and paste it into Microsoft Word. The text all pasted normally except for the very last line, which was highlighted and which Yvette certainly hadn't written. It read, "Enjoy the View."

Yvette went back to check her sent emails. She wondered if she had maybe replied to an old email and copied text from an earlier email chain. But no. She had sent a brand new email and the line, "Enjoy the View" had not been in it.

There's probably an ordinary reality explanation for this. But Yvette most definitely does get a birds eye view from the work she does with so many different people. It seems that, no matter what anyone is going through, no matter how alone they feel, someone else is working through something similar too. We honestly and truly are all in this together.

DEEPENING INTO THE DREAM

One night, Yvette had a dream of a plant and of a person. Soon after, the person Yvette had dreamed of asked Yvette to do some journey work for her.

Within the journey that followed, Yvette was given the name of a plant to give to that person. When Yvette looked the plant up on the internet, it looked like the plant of her dream. She also found out that it did have a healing use that could be of benefit. What's more, the person had just happened to come across the exact same plant within their own shamanic work.

Little synchronicities to do with plants gathered pace and Yvette began to feel as though a future body of work to do with plants was beginning to take shape.

As the hour of a Full Moon Eclipse drew near, in Pisces, the sign which most easily dreams, Yvette was taken over by an urge to find and connect with a plant known to help dreamers, Artemisia Vulgaris, or more commonly, Mugwort. Her biggest problems included the following facts: she didn't know what the plant looked like, she didn't know where to find it, and she didn't know if it could easily be confused with any other plants. Furthermore, if it could be confused with other plants, she didn't know if these other plants could be dangerous.

Her google trail eventually led her to the website of a group of medical herbalists. Yvette called the number, leaving a half-hearted voice message, not expecting to hear back. To her surprise, she was called back very quickly. The lady she spoke to was so lovely and kind, she took the time to tell Yvette all about the plant and where to find it. There was something in that lady's voice that was so warm and familiar, it made Yvette feel that, if she didn't know this woman already, she really wanted to.

The lady told Yvette that she would most definitely be able to find this plant on a road in Hertfordshire. She would even have been so happy to come out and show Yvette herself but she was, coincidentally, teaching a workshop in Dorset, just around the corner from the Sacred Trust.

Yvette parked on a little road, just off the road she'd been directed to. As she climbed out of her car, she saw a plant straight away which looked like Artemisia Vulgaris. Unsure, she continued to the road she'd been told of and walked up and down the road, looking for the plant but she did not see anything like it.

She went back to the plant she'd first seen and, still unsure, she took some of it home where she planted it and spent some time with it. All the way home, the songs on the radio were full of references to do with the Moon. The next day, Yvette saw a client for shamanic healing whose name was Diane, a name which has links with the Goddess of the Moon.

After all that and a few days later, Yvette went to stay with a friend she'd met on one of the Path of Pollen training courses at the Sacred Trust. This friend seemed to have a really good knowledge of plants, had Artemisia in abundance and made Yvette some tea with it. Her friend even knew the medical herbalist Yvette had called as she had met her when they had also done some of the Path of Pollen work together some time before.

Yvette later learned from the medical herbalist that the plant she'd gathered was indeed Artemisia. She certainly had interesting dreams with the plant but she has interesting dreams anyway. What interested her most were the mysteries in the ways of the Moon, the women, the bees and in the ways of those who work with the bees which seemed to have brought them all together.

MERCURY RETROGRADE

All the planets in the universe are moved by their own song and each of these songs has its own tempo. We are lucky enough to watch, from our position here on Earth, some of this planetary dance around the Sun. We are also lucky enough to know that a lot of what we see isn't truly taking place in the way in which we see it.

One of the things we see is the apparent backward movement of a planet through our skies. Have you ever been on a train travelling alongside another train which is moving at a different speed to the train that you are on? If so, you will have seen what it looks like to watch a forward moving object look like it is going backwards. But you know it isn't really. That's the same idea behind the planets moving backwards through our skies.

This apparent backward movement of the planet is called retrograde motion. Each planet, except the Moon (which circles the Earth rather than the Sun,) goes retrograde at some point. (Astrologers refer to the Moon as a planet for simplicity's sake, we know it isn't really a planet.)

Many, many years ago, our ancestors started watching the stars and they started to notice the patterns of events that corresponded with particular planetary events. They figured out which topics go with which planets. They also figured out how well, or how badly, things to do with these topics would go when certain things were happening with the planet.

Mercury, they saw, had to do with thought and communication, with travel, stories, actors, siblings, sales, neighbours, thieves, hands, arms, lungs, to name but a few. To 'name something' is of Mercury. Words.

Our ancestors also noticed that, around three times a year, when Mercury went retrograde, very little success happened in any of these areas that go with Mercury and, in fact, things to do with these areas were more than likely to go very wrong.

Nowadays, when Mercury is getting ready to step backwards through our skies, the internet is full of warnings which speak of difficulties to do with anything which comes under Mercury's domain: foggy thinking, misunderstandings, breakdowns of cars, computer problems and so forth.

Many people fearfully prepare themselves for the worst, while many others stoically resign themselves to a period of frustration. Some people will altogether avoid having anything to do with any of Mercury's areas during this time.

One day, Yvette was chatting with her Allies about her dream vocation, when she asked, "But Mercury is retrograde. Can I still start this now?" As part of their response, Yvette's Allies invited Mercury to step into the conversation. When he reminded her, it just seemed so obvious. Of course! He is Hermes. He is Thoth. Thoth who brought us magic and writing. He is a Deity of Psychopomp, helping newly deceased souls travel from this world into the next. He is a Messenger of the Gods and he is the only God with the freedom to move between all the worlds.

It seemed to Yvette as though it could be Mercury then who would also be able to move freely between the objective reality of Science and the subjective reality of Astrology.

Yvette thought of the magic which explains that, in order for something to exist in this physical reality, it much first exist in another reality. She thought about how often Simon would repeat the astrologer, Caroline Casey's, phrase, "Imagination lays the tracks for the reality train to follow." She thought about how very much this fits in with Mercury and his domain: imagination, thoughts, words.

She began to wonder, "When things go wrong during a retrograde, are they really going wrong or are they just appearing to go wrong?" Her answer came in the form of an email from a friend of hers who knows nothing of astrology or of Mercury Retrogrades or of what to worry about when they're happening. This friend of hers told her he had been reading a very long email that Yvette had sent to him. While he had been trying to read her email, his computer kept shutting down. This, he said, had meant he had had to read her email a number of times. This in turn, he said, had meant he had truly absorbed what it was that she had been trying to tell him. What he then went on to say to her was more rich and deeper in content than usual, and Yvette has no doubt that this conversation has nourished the friendship between them.

The more she hung out with Mercury, the more she began to understand that the time when he goes backwards, the time when his energy is directed within rather than without, is a magically rich time. She found it to be a time during which the field of potential is particularly ripe for being planted with new ideas and thoughts which can then go on to take shape in our external, shared world.

She thought about all the information the astrologers before her had gathered about Mercury Retrograde. Feeling so very grateful to them for the body of knowledge they had made available to her, she began to consider it some more.

In the days of yore, astrology was almost solely applied to nations. As the ruling sovereign was considered to be linked to the well-being of the nation, astrology was also applied to the King or to the Queen. She asked herself, when the astrologers had looked at what was going on, had they been assessing affairs against what they wanted them to be, rather than considering or assessing them against what they could have been, given our innate ability to create?

She began to understand, that when things to do with Mercury went badly during a retrograde, one of two things were happening. It could be that people were reaping the fruits of some very effective magic in that what they had been thinking had come to pass. Or it could be that people were receiving a communication from Mercury who was trying to draw their attention to the fact that something in what they were doing needed correcting or improving.

Yvette went on to share her findings with others. She was careful to make sure they understood that this way of working with this retrograde time was a working with Mercury and an honouring of a Deity rather than the winning of a battle or the overcoming of a long held tradition. She was careful to remind them to thank Mercury for all that he does for us too.

Since then, Yvette has gone on to reap the rewards of this approach and to see others do the same. She's seen unsolicited help arrive to repair all sorts of items that had long since been damaged in a home while Mercury was going backwards in the fourth house of the person's chart. The fourth house has to do with, among other things, the home.

She's seen tax rebates when Mercury retrograded through an eighth house of the person's chart. The eighth house has to do with, among other things, tax.

She's seen a friend, having saved and saved, fulfil a lifelong dream to go to the USA during a Mercury Retrograde where, for the first time, she drove a car on the other side of the road. On that road trip, during that Mercury Retrograde, her friend travelled, incident free, for close to 2,500 miles.

She's seen people plan trips during a Mercury Retrograde and successfully carry them out during the following Retrograde. She's seen all sorts of other things that have to do with Mercury go well during a Mercury Retrograde.

Yvette's own car, which she still enjoys to this day, was bought at a very good price during a Mercury Retrograde. She has even travelled, incident free, all the way from London to the South of France and back again, in this car during the pre-shadow period of the Mercury Retrograde, a time just before he goes backwards and which is seen to share the dangers of the retrograde.

One day, while Mercury was retrograde, Yvette was walking towards her car because she was about to drive to Wales. She passed a man on the side of the road. He was replacing the tyre on his car while a number of young boys surrounded him, reciting instructions on the next step in the changing of tyres. At the time, she thought to herself, "Hmm. I know exactly what the people who believe that Mercury Retrograde is bad would have to say about this."

Almost four hundred, incident free, miles later, Yvette spent the first evening of her holiday in a lovely little spot in the middle of Wales. The next day, she continued onward for another sixty, incident free, miles to the North of Wales, easily finding the spots she'd wanted to see along the way.

When she arrived in Conwy, she discovered she had left her telephone charger in the middle of Wales. "Hmm," she thought, "Telephone interrupted. This is the stuff of Mercury Retrograde."

She thought she understood she was receiving a warning. She had increasingly been feeling as though she herself were battery to her phone, her life force draining from her as, every few minutes, she habitually checked it and absorbed whatever advertisement or uninteresting piece of news was there. She knows better than this. It was clear to her that she needed to adjust this habit.

Someone at the place she was staying at gave her a telephone charger to use.

Having spent a couple of days in the North of Wales, driving all over and hearing wonderful stories and meeting wonderful people, Yvette headed south. She stopped en route and spent some time at what may or may not have been the grave of Taliesin. (She found the spot all right, it's just that it hasn't been proven that it is definitely his grave.) Just as she was leaving, she noticed an email from a friend of hers pop up on her phone.

As she continued southwards, she stopped at Devil's Bridge where she realised she could no longer find her phone. Three things made her believe her phone could be lost:

Firstly, she couldn't find it. Secondly, she thought she could remember having heard something which could have been her phone dropping to the ground when she had climbed into her car back at Taliesin's could be grave. Thirdly, knowing her phone had been almost fully charged, her car radio which was linked to her phone, could not detect it.

A couple of things told her not to worry: She hadn't looked very hard for it. She wondered if she would even replace her phone if it did turn out to be lost as she certainly hadn't replaced her habits in the days that had followed her leaving her charger behind her in the middle of Wales.

Yet, still, she continued to refer to her phone as temporarily or as potentially lost. Both when she arrived at her friend's house some one hundred, incident free, miles later and when she (successfully) emailed other people who might be wanting to contact her while she was away.

Now based at her friends in the South of Wales, Yvette spent a day seeing some more of the sights that Wales has to offer. She had been on the hunt for a lake which has strong links with a famous mythical female. Just as she'd finally drawn close to this lake, she realised that, the entire time she'd been trying to work out where the lake was, the Moon had been hanging over the spot as though it had been trying to show her the way.

Enchanted by this Moon, Yvette kept an eye on it as she began to drive back to her friend's house. It began to glow brighter and brighter as the evening sky darkened and, very soon, the Moon was accompanied by Venus, sparkling brightly at her side. Yvette had half an eye on the road and the rest of her being focused on the night sky and on the spots where she might be able to stop to take pictures of this sky. Suddenly, her tyre bumped into one of the rocks which had been placed on the side of the road, presumably to prevent drivers from careening over the edge.

This, she thought to herself, was a very sharp warning to pay attention to the road while driving. She stopped at a nearby garage where she saw that her tyre was flat. Without a phone and without the skills to change her tyre (I know,) she asked the shopkeeper for advice. The shopkeeper offered to help but could not locate the jack within the car and so, he looked up the number for roadside assistance and lent Yvette the use of his phone so that she could call for help.

It was, apparently, a very busy night in Wales - the wait for assistance would be up to four hours! Sitting in her car, Yvette spent some of the time writing some of the stories that you are reading now.

Suddenly, she thought to herself, "This is just too much!" First the phone charger, then the phone. Then the car tyre, and now the long wait for assistance to arrive. She thought she'd understood the warnings with the phone charger and the phone. She thought she'd understood the warning to do with her driving. She'd thought it wasn't Mercury, the Moon, Venus or anyone's fault other than her own that she hadn't been watching where she was going.

However, this was all stuff of the traditional interpretation of Mercury Retrograde. She didn't even have the number of the friends she was staying with to let them know she'd be so late home. More stuff of Mercury Retrograde. Was she being stubborn? Had she been wrong in her understanding of how to use this time? Had she advised others in a way which was perhaps unhelpful or even harmful to them?

With her beloved drum in the car and suspecting she had more time to spare as the four hours were not yet up, she journeyed to her Allies to find out more. When she arrived, Mercury was with them. "What's going on," she pleaded? "Have I got things so very wrong?" They assured her and reassured her, the direction in which she and Mercury were travelling was sound and, even though he is also known as a trickster, this was not, they said, a case of Mercury playing a trick on her.

When she asked about her lost phone, they wrote down on paper, "Song. Change your song." She struggled to understand this and so she asked about her tyre. They told her to take heed, it had been a warning to drive safely. When she asked about the assistance which still hadn't arrived, they promised her it would arrive soon and she would not be spending the cold night out there alone and without a phone. Again, Mercury promised Yvette, he was her Ally and she could trust him.

No more than ten minutes later, the assistance man arrived. He enquired after the whereabouts of a little tool Yvette had never heard of before. The tool was specific to her own car and was needed to remove the tyre. Well. Yvette's car had not been tidy to begin with and was now cluttered with all sorts from her travels around Wales. They searched and they searched, but they could not find it. The man did, however, find Yvette's phone. Ah! Change your song! It was the wrong question as the phone wasn't lost.

Rather unusually, the man had arrived in a vehicle which was able carry another car and so, having paid a hefty amount for having to be towed for more than ten miles, Yvette was taken home without having to make another call out. The next morning, Yvette found the tool they'd been looking for and her friend's partner changed her tyre for her.

She later thought about how her holiday had started with

68

someone replacing a tyre and had ended with her having to replace her own. Had Mercury already been warning her to drive safely back then? She thought about the little boys reciting instructions on how to change a tyre. Had Mercury been warning her to learn how to change her tyre? She thought about the lost phone in her car and she wondered, had Mercury been trying to tell her there was something missing in her car? Had he been warning her to tidy it up?

She thought about how her last day had begun with the sighting of a fox, one of her oldest and dearest Allies, on the top of a hill associated with stories of Myrddin. She thought about the way the day had ended with another sighting of a fox that had dashed across a traffic circle in the middle of the night as that nice man from roadside assistance had taken Yvette home. This may not seem unusual to you, as people are constantly telling Yvette that they see foxes all the time. Yvette doesn't. For her, it's a rare and special occasion which always leaves her feeling as though she has had an encounter with an otherworldly creature who is distinctively wise and distinctively magical.

She thought about how lucky she is to have Fox in her life. She thought about how he sometimes reminds her of Gemini - that curious, youthful, fun loving sign, sometimes mortal and sometimes immortal - which comes under the rulership of Mercury. She thought about how lucky she is to have Mercury as one of her friends and she thought about how lucky she is to get to know him and all of the other planets as well as all of the other signs through using these shamanic ways. Had Mercury, with the help of Fox, already been reminding her of his support? Was he telling her not to doubt him or their friendship?

She thought about how much she looks forward to spending however many days she is lucky enough to have left - be they retrograde days or not - to go deeper and deeper and deeper still into all the wonders that these ways have to offer. She is quite clear that there is no planet or planetary activity which can be any more evil or foreboding than anything else which is natural in our world - the sunshine, the rain, the snow and the like.

Like lots of people, she's wary of phrases that begin with, "They say," but she does agree with 'them' when 'they say,' "There's no bad weather. Only bad clothes."

THE LEGENDS OF THE LAND

Yvette was on holiday when a man at the place where she was staying told her a story. Legend has it, this man began, that there is a hill called Dinas Emrys where the ruler of the land, Vortigern, had been trying to build a fortress as protection against the threat of the Saxons. The fortress kept crumbling. A young boy called Myrddin told Vortigern that beneath the hill there lay a lake and in that lake there were two dragons. The one dragon was white and the other dragon was red. Vortigern went on to find a lake in that hill and the dragons were awoken. The dragons fought and, although the red dragon appeared to be the weaker of the two, it was the red dragon who won. Myrddin explained that the red dragon represented the people of Briton who would prevail while the white dragon represented the Saxons.

When Yvette saw that it was possible for her to get to this place from the place where she was, she just had to go and visit. She left one very early morning and, as she drove up and down the road, she just couldn't see any hill which looked like the hill she'd seen when she'd looked it up on the internet.

She stopped to ask an old couple who assured her she had just passed the hill she was seeking. They told her that she would have a better view of the hill if she walked around the lake on the opposite side of the road.

By this time, Yvette desperately wanted to see this hill. As she walked around the lake, she felt herself beginning to call to the Spirits of the Land and to her Allies. She pleaded with them, "Please show me what to do."

She looked down and she noticed she was wearing a black top and a red skirt that she'd hardly ever worn before. The absence of white in her outfit struck her as being out of balance with the place. At the same time as she had noticed this, the words, "Awaken the red dragon!" sounded authoritatively in her head. For one brief, terrifying moment, Yvette wondered if she was evil - what was she doing having anything to do with an awakening of a red dragon?! Suddenly, flooded with relief, she remembered that the red dragon was the good guy in Wales.

She glanced back over her shoulder and saw a unmistakable flash of red running across the hilltop. As she remained, transfixed, gazing upon that hilltop, the red on the hilltop deepened and grew into the shape of a serpent like dragon.

After some time, she continued along the road to look for a lake that had to do with stories of ladies and of lakes when she met a lady serving coffee at a little shop on the side of the road. The lady told Yvette a story about a little village called Beddgelert.

"Beddgelert," said the lady, "Means the grave of Gelert." And she went on to tell the story of how Beddgelert got its name.

There once was a man who had a baby. He also had a dog named Gelert. One day, the man told his dog to look after his baby and, while the man was out, the dog and the baby were attacked by a wolf. But the little dog fought back. And, somehow, the little dog won.

When the man returned home and he saw the remains of a fight and of a kill, he thought the worst for his baby. In his rage and in his grief, he avenged his beloved baby by killing his beloved dog. When he saw his little baby was alive and well, the man realised how brave his little dog must have been to have won.

Overcome with remorse for what he had done, he placed his little dog in his final resting place. It is the strength of this man's love and the strength of his remorse which keeps the memory of his little dog's name alive, still to this day.

Yvette has since journeyed to ask, "What does it mean to awaken the red dragon?" She wrote her question down amongst a series of other questions, blindfolded herself and picked one up so she wouldn't know what she was journeying on at the time.

In Yvette's journey, she moved out from her body and out through the front door of her home, where a Deity Yvette loves to work with picked Yvette up into her arms. The Deity helped Yvette up into a new place which she had never visited before. The ground was natural and there was water. A dark ship sailed in from the darkness. It had a ladder on its side. Yvette climbed up the ladder into the ship. The ship sailed back off into the dark and, in Yvette's journey, she felt as though she had disappeared. Suddenly, a light turned on, revealing a tiny old man who looked exactly like the character Engywook in the film, The Never Ending Story. He was poring over his books, studying the Sphinx Gate which, in the film, saw so many heroes die. Yvette asked, "It's not me who has to go through that gate?" 'Engywook' carried on looking at his book. He got up and went to a little shelf which was filled with vials. He selected one and gave it to Yvette. It was filled with old, white stuff. After some guesses as to what it might be, 'Engywook' nodded that, yes, it was turnip. Yvette ate some of the turnip and was shown that she was now to run through the Sphinx Gate. She did so, successfully, but when she looked back there was nothing there and Yvette was back with the Deity with whom her journey had begun.

Yvette is sure that the meaning of this journey will take some time to unfold. She knows the Sphinx Gate has to do with the courage of the heart. She knows her courage was fed by something white which grows in the Earth. She knows she was comforted by the nothingness that was behind her and by the Deity who was with her at both the beginning and at the end.

She knows that her mother is still with her.

She's fairly certain that, when she visited Dinas Emrys, she found the right hill and, even though she's not yet sure what it means, she knows that the red dragon is awake. She knows that the red dragon is within her and she knows that its awakening is good.

WELCOME TO MY WORLD

PART ONE: THE GRATEFUL DEAD

Almost every week, for over a year, a friend and I have been working together to help deceased souls transcend to the place where they really need to go so that they can continue on to do what they need to do. It is beautiful and fulfilling work. The visions my friend and I have shared with each other seem to hold blessings for the dead, for the living and for the land.

It certainly feels as though, at the very least, this work holds blessings for my own soul. Both today and tomorrow.

One evening, after having been obsessed by a song by the artist called Prince, I was reading up about him on the internet. I learned of his childhood vision of an angel which told him he would no longer suffer from epileptic fits. I learned of his own approach to art and of his own deep spirituality. The more I read about him as a person, the more I liked him.

My google trail eventually led me to the Rolling Stone Magazine's list of the Top 100 Artists. I cannot even describe the beautiful feeling that filled me from outside in and from inside out, when I was suddenly showered in tingles and, seconds later, I scrolled down to land upon the entry for the band called "The Grateful Dead."

I can't help but notice that Prince, who led me to this synchronicity, was also, for a while, known by a symbol which is made up of the symbols of Venus and Mars, those same symbols I encountered in my pilgrimage story.

And my blessing for tomorrow? I'm not worried about dying. I know where I am going, as I have been there before, and I know who will be there to welcome me.

PART TWO: AN ANCIENT YEW TREE

I once approached one of the Great Yews of these Blessed Isles. I took a few photographs and then went to rest my hand upon its trunk. "Get Off!" The words were so quick and so sharp, I felt they could actually have stung me.

Surely I must have made this up? I had never experienced anything but nourishment, replenishment, love and support whenever I had spent some time with nature. I went to touch the tree again. "Get off, get off!" Again, so quickly, so sharply and then gone.

"Wow," I wondered, "What had I done?" Perhaps it was because I had taken photographs before greeting the tree, or without having asked the tree for permission?

A couple of ladies came out of the adjacent church. I asked them about their yew tree and, as one of the ladies led me around the trunk, the other lady gasped in awe, having never seen the magnificence of that side of the tree before. A gentleman who had been in the graveyard approached, wanting to know what it was that we had discovered. He too circled the tree, admiring it from that angle for what seemed like the very first time. They wondered if the Yew Tree had been there for long and whether it had been there before the church had been built. I shared with them what I knew of Yew Trees and of Yew Trees in churchyards.

These people had walked past this yew tree so often and they had not even realised the treasure they had with them right there in their midst. They were such lovely people, they even invited me, a lone traveller and a stranger to them, to go and have dinner with them that night.

I spoke with the Yew Tree again and it seemed that the tree had forgotten how special and sacred it was. It had forgotten its purpose and how it had been revered so many thousands of years ago. As I told it what I knew of the yews, we bonded.

It may well be that this event took place in this way because, within that one moment in time, something needed to take place between the tree, those people and I. And it may be that what took place helped us all. Perhaps if you went and honoured this tree or any other that you're drawn to, you would have your own and different story to tell.

PART THREE: AWAKENING TO THE ROCKS

One day, I visited a place with some rocks which had been standing there for over six thousand years.

At first, the rocks told me they didn't really want me there. They told me that I was as dead to them as they were to me. "Well, how are we to awaken to each other?" I asked.

After some time, sitting in silence, there arose within me the remembrance that we both came from dust. A feeling of companionship grew between us; they showed me their faces and we chatted a while.

I left them with a strong bond intact between us. The world I live in is, after all, mine. Why on earth (excuse the pun) would I not want to connect to it?

PART FOUR: MY FRIEND WHO LECTURES AT OXFORD UNIVERSITY

He's so cool.

I first met him at university just after I had finished school. At that time, I had held a lifelong fear of being locked up for being insane. If this ever did happen to me, I didn't know how I would ever be able to convince anyone that I was sane.

In one short conversation, my friend showed me why I didn't need to worry.

With him, I can say whatever it is that I would like to say. With him, I can ask whatever it is that I would like to ask. Even on the most sensitive of topics. He doesn't judge. He just listens and he answers my questions. He can see where I am coming from and I can see where he is coming from.

He doesn't believe in astrology and he doesn't believe in shamanism. But when I told him I had written a book, he became the very first person who has said to me, "I'll buy it."

PART FIVE: THE PERSON WHO FIRST TOLD ME ABOUT THE SACRED TRUST

Is still laughing at me.

I first met her on a psychic development course. When she told me about the Sacred Trust and the Darkness Visible workshop they run, which she so desperately wanted to do, I laughed and said, "Come and visit me. I'll turn out the lights, you can pay me for it and I will save on electricity."

It must have been because I was so impressed by her abilities on that course that I went on to attend the Sacred Trust's introduction to shamanism. In the years that followed, I devoured every single thing that the Sacred Trust had to offer.

Every time I came back from the training, singing, "I learned this," and, "I learned that," my friend laughed and said, "But do you remember what you said when I first told you about the Sacred Trust?"

Yes, Magda. I remember.

And when I told her I had written a book, she became the second person to say to me, "I'll buy it."

(P.S. While writing this, I remembered that, when I was a little girl, I would never tell anyone my mother's maiden name. It's the beginning to most South African jokes. I realised that both my mother's first name and Magda's name can be associated with the name, Mary. It felt as though, in some strange way, my mother 'is still laughing at me' too!)

PART SIX: A CYCLONE NAMED YVETTE

One day, I was arguing with my friend. I was becoming angrier and angrier. My point was important to me and I just couldn't understand why she couldn't see where I was coming from. I kept journeying to my Allies on what to do and they kept warning me to be careful. My journeys told me I was in danger of becoming dangerous.

My friend and I were due to spend some time together, but we were no closer to seeing eye to eye. So I cancelled our plans (yes, the Christmas ones) and the anger vanished.

At around the same time, I did a healing for another friend. When I told this person of the journeys I done for her and of the violent storms I had encountered within them, she asked me if I'd heard of the cyclone named Yvette. I hadn't and so I looked it up.

I read on the news that there was indeed a cyclone named Yvette. The news said that the cyclone had started to form on the very same day that my friend and I had started arguing. What's more, I read that on the same day that I had excused myself from our plans, the severity of the cyclone had been downgraded. Had the cyclone not lost its power, it was on track to strike land at a place called... You guessed it! (Although my friend's name is a shortened version of this name.)

Of course, I don't believe that my anger created that cyclone. Shamanism is about healing and the restoration of balance. The Shaman knows that 'the intent sets the trajectory' and I'd certainly had no intent of creating a cyclone. There was another time when I had just finished a journey in which I had moved forwards and backwards in time when a friend of mine posted on facebook that her clock, in ordinary reality, had just been moving forwards and backwards in time. I don't think that I made her clock do that either.

What I do know is that Spirit sends me messages all the time and that, the more I listen, the clearer they become. I think Spirit was telling me it's ok as I'd been feeling guilty about cancelling the Christmas plans. I think Spirit was telling me I had been wise to cancel our plans and to get out of a situation in which I couldn't resolve my anger. When I later spoke to Simon about something else entirely, I think Spirit was telling me something then too. In that conversation, Simon had been emphasizing the importance of resolution.

Of course my friend and I will resolve this. We love each other dearly. She's always the first to volunteer when I need to practice something I've just learned, so it's fitting that she lets me practice resolving things on her too.

(P.S. When I sent this section to her to check if she had any concerns about possibly being identifiable within this, she replied within minutes. She said I could spell her name out if I wanted to and she suggested I replace the word 'dearly' with unconditionally ☺

PART SEVEN: UNRAVELLING SOME THINGS THAT HAVE GONE WRONG

One day, just after we'd been taught how to unravel certain types of wrongs that we've done or had done to us, I journeyed to find out which of my clients would most benefit from this work.

As I usually do, I had written down a number of questions on a number of pieces of paper. I'd blindfolded myself and selected a question, so I didn't know which question I was journeying on.

In my journey, I met with the Goddess Gaia. We danced together and then, holding hands, we watched the ground as something began to grow. It turned into a plant and, on that plant, there were all sorts of shapes which held all sorts of meanings. When I turned the question over to see what I had journeyed on, I understood that I was to unravel something that had gone wrong for the Earth.

In the healing work that followed, I went on a journey of the most epic proportions. Gaia came with me and, when we came to a volcano which I must always pass, Gaia showed me I was to carry on without her.

My journey took me up through many levels where I encountered many scenes. Eventually, I came to an enormous set of double doors. They opened before me and I was face to face with a giant sun. I stared at this bright sun for quite some time until, eventually, the Gods of the Sun stepped forward. They were blowing sunlight filled kisses down onto the Earth.

With the journey now over, I went out into the woodland where I live. The light coming through the trees formed pools of sunlight on the ground which looked so vivid, I could imagine diving into them. Four days later, I heard for the first time via an article a friend posted on facebook that the ozone layer was healing. The only thing which was hindering this healing was volcanic activity. No wonder Gaia stayed at the volcano in my journey!

Of course, I don't believe my afternoon's journey work is responsible for the millions of people who have worked hard – whether in ordinary reality or in non-ordinary reality – to bring this healing of the ozone layer about. It's a synchronicity. Its meaning will be more subtle than A causes B and its meaning may well never be revealed. But when I journeyed to try to find out more, I had a sense of a great and loving Spiritual being. And even though, in my journey, this being was far, far away, it seemed to want this world to be whole and it seemed to be saying that it will work with those of us who, in the depths of our hearts, want this world to be whole too.

PART ∞: THE BEES

One day, my friend, who keeps bees, told me that, over the previous weekend, he had unexpectedly been given another four hives. I was amazed. That same weekend, I had attended a Path of Pollen course at the Sacred Trust where we had carried out a ceremony to bless the bees.

There are other little synchronicities which tell me that this blessing is multiplying too. Everything we do, in whatever capacity we can do it, can have a very real impact on the well-being of the bees. It is so important that we do everything that is in our power to make sure that the bees do thrive.

The impact the bees have on our survival is obvious. It's more than enough of an argument to do what we can for them. Even without considering the myths and the legends associated with the bees; even without considering bee shamanism (whose outer edges I've only just begun to touch,) looking after the bees looks like it could be the single most important thing we can do in our lives.

AFTERWORD

I did contact Mr Brewer again. When he checked my name which I had just given to him, he said, "Marks? As in top marks?"

Anyone who knows me well will know how much this made me smile. I awoke the next morning thinking that, as much as I am grateful to my mother for the name she has given to me, I am grateful to my father for the surname he has given to me too.

ANOTHER AFTERWORD

Simon Buxton, I will never forget that, when I told you I had
written stories, you said you looked forward to reading them, but did
not need to see them before they were published.

Siegfried Marks, I will never forget that, when I told you I had
written stories, you also said you looked forward to reading them, but
did not need to see them before they were published.

Jerome Salyers, I will never forget that time when you explained
the difference between trust and an assumption to me. The answer is
only obvious when you know it!

(P.S. I hope what I am trying to say here is clear, Jerome didn't ask
to see the book either.)

PS: ∞

Having finished writing these stories, I sat on my couch with my blindfold on and a number of little papers with questions written upon them by my side.

As the drumming began, I rose up and left my body. In this non ordinary reality, I looked down and I could see I was wearing a skirt. I gathered the flowing fabric into my hands, raising it above my bare legs. My awareness moved out of this non ordinary version of myself and I watched the rest of the scene unfold much as one might watch a film.

In the blink of an eye, I found myself standing in a shallow river. The weather was calm and the waters were clear. I leaned forward, looking into the waters where I saw many fish and many treasures. I wondered to myself, "How had I got here?" I hadn't used my usual route.

I began to wash myself with the waters. I started with my legs and I continued up my arms. My skin began to glow. When I got to my head, I could see that it was a skeleton. I wondered if this was the face of my Ancestors and the head began to nod, "Yes." The Body, I realised, is linked with the Ancestors and, together, we were washing in these waters.

I asked, "Is there anything else you can tell me?" The hand moved up to point to the ear, gesturing, "Listen." As I said, "Am I to listen?" the head nodded and the hand began to trace the lemniscate in the air.

In ordinary reality, my telephone rang and so I came back.

When I took off my blindfold and I turned my question over, I read, "Is there anything Mama needs me to do which I am not doing now?" I'd asked this question as, over the previous few days, I'd had the sense that my mother was trying to tell me something.

A few hours later, I made the acquaintance of a very interesting man and I listened very carefully as he told me some very, very interesting things. I listened as he told me story after story and fact after fact. Hours later, I was still sitting in my living room, staring straight ahead, stunned by what he had said.

And of what he told me? There's something Simon once said to me which created no small amount of internal tension for me. I am sorry but I'm going to borrow his words again now.

He said, "Wait and see." ☺

∞

AND AN EPILOGUE

In case you don't know anything about shamanism, or, in case I use the words related to shamanism in a different way to the that way you do, here's a bit about what I know about shamanism.

The Shaman performs many functions with the main objective being healing or the restoration of balance. When I speak of shamanism here, I am using the language of core shamanism, developed by Michael Harner who is an anthropologist and who is recognised as a Shaman by the many indigenous Shamans with whom he has worked across the world.

Core shamanism is a body of knowledge which brings together those practices and principles to do with shamanism which are universal or near universal. That is to say, they have been found to exist cross culturally.

Within each hunter gatherer society, there is a person who performs a certain function. This function is similar across cultures and there are many similarities in the ways in which this function is performed. The anthropologists borrowed the word Shaman to describe it. The word 'Shaman' comes from the Tungus people of Siberia. Other societies have other names for it.

For some time, the anthropologists wondered whether it might be that this role is so similar and performed so similarly across the globe because, once upon a time, there was a Shaman somewhere and this Shaman taught other Shamans and it then spread out. They decided that this was unlikely, particularly given how much things like language and family structure have changed as they spread. It seems more likely that societies across the globe had, independently of one another, discovered or uncovered certain truths.

And what are these truths? The Shaman knows that there is more than this world which we can see, feel and touch. The Shaman knows that there is also a Spiritual Reality. Everything that is - the chair that I'm sitting on, this pen with which I'm writing and so forth has a Spirit.

The Shaman has a map of this Spiritual Reality. Like maps of our Physical Reality, it is only a map. In this map of the Spiritual Reality, the Shaman speaks of an Upper World, a Middle World and a Lower World which exist outside of time and space. The Upper Worlds and the Lower Worlds are places where the Shaman meets with divine, loving, transcended, compassionate beings who only want to help us. In the Upper World, these beings are, typically, encountered in human or humanoid form and in the Lower World they are, typically, encountered in animal form. We say typically because, the Shaman knows, there are no rules.

The Middle World is a Spiritual double to our Physical Reality. It includes the Spirit of the Chair I'm sitting on and the Spirit of my Pen with which I'm writing. It also includes the Spirits of the Trees, the Rocks and the Sand. And so on. The Spirits of the Middle World are not the same as the divine, loving, compassionate, transcended beings of the Upper Worlds and the Lower Worlds who only want to help us. The Spirit of the Tree, for example, a Middle World Spirit, has the interests of the Trees at heart. Furthermore, it may not have the same morality as you and I. Having said that, I wouldn't want to give the impression that the Shaman doesn't work with these spirits. The Shaman does - the Spirits of the Middle World can be extraordinarily helpful. The Shaman also knows that Nature is the visible face of spirit and cares passionately about the well-being of this planet.

The Middle World is the place where the Shaman can also find the unquiet dead, those souls of the deceased who have not yet managed to get to where they need to go so that they can continue on their journey, whether that's to the Upper Worlds, the Lower Worlds or somewhere else.

The Shaman moves purposefully between the Physical Realities and the Spiritual Realities. I say purposefully, because the Shaman goes to the places they go to with an intent. The Shaman doesn't go there by accident and the Shaman has a reason for going there.

The Shaman moves between these Worlds, the Physical and the Spiritual, by changing his/her state of consciousness. Just as we have a waking state of consciousness, a day dreaming state of consciousness, a sleeping state of consciousness and so forth, we also have a shamanic state of consciousness. The shamanic state of consciousness allows the Shaman to move from an 'ordinary reality' waking state in Physical Reality, into the 'non-ordinary' Spiritual Reality. There are many ways of changing this state of consciousness - singing, dancing, taking mind altering substances and so forth. The way I have been taught is through drumming as this is a "core" method found across cultures. The drum is also sometimes called the 'Shaman's Horse.' The brain waves follow the rhythm of the drum (which is sounded at a specific rhythm and at a specific pace) into a shamanic state of consciousness.

We call this movement of ourselves from this Physical Reality into the Spiritual Reality a 'shamanic journey' or 'journey' for short. The journey feels like a day dream and it can feel like the person journeying is making it up. The person journeying soon finds out that they are most definitely not making it up. This is based on the information they receive and the very real impact their journeys have on their ordinary realities. The Spiritual Reality is a non consensual reality. The Shaman makes many friends in the Spiritual Realities and the Shaman knows that these friends are our Allies, our True Teachers.

The reason for going to these Spiritual Realities is primarily for healing, most especially the restoration of balance. We work in partnership with the Spirits to give effect to this healing. The Spirits are divine, loving, compassionate, transcended beings (or not when we work with them in the Middle World) but they are not all powerful. We have free will. Which is why we work in partnership with them.

This free will is sacred and this is why I will never, ever do any healing for you or for anyone else without your/their permission.

The healing is carried out in many ways and is done on the behalf of many different beings. Most importantly, we start with ourselves. I am seeking to become whole (not perfect, but whole) with the understanding that the more I work on myself, the more what is around me will be healed.

The Shaman also works with other humans, with ancestors, with nature and so on. The Shaman also acts as psychopomp, helping the unquiet dead get to the places where they need to go so that they can continue on to do what they need to do.

"What is it like to engage with shamanism and shamanic practices?" you may wonder. I can't tell you that. You have to experience it for yourself. There are just as many ways as there are many people in this world but it is a pathway of Direct Revelation. There are people who might be able to show you the way, but the True Teachers are the Spirits you engage with.

ABOUT THE AUTHOR

My insatiable interest in being a human has led me to all sorts of studies, all sorts of places and to all sorts of people.

I love music, stories and travelling. I can be as difficult as the most difficult of you, I'm sure, but I love the feeling that I get from being nice too.

I've studied Psychology, Astrology, the Tarot, the Runes and various systems of energetic healing. For me, personally, it is the practice of shamanic techniques which has brought it all together and which has lit everything up.

I am passionate about healing and about our innate creative abilities that can be used to draw very real and lasting changes into our lives. If there is anyone out there who is struggling and who could be helped by receiving shamanic healing, I really want them to know that this type of healing exists.

Whoever you are and whatever your sacred dream is (that goal of yours which is untainted by ego or by the expectations of others) I want you to be helped to achieve this. It doesn't matter what this dream is, whether it's to sweep the streets or to provide healthcare for others, I believe that, for every step that anyone takes towards fulfilling their dream, the rest of us reaps the rewards (provided, of course, that the step's taken without hindering the dreams of others.)

I agree with my teacher when he says, "Labels are for bottles, not people." But here is a label I do like: Aspiring Shaman. When I say the words, they flow out on my breath but my entire body feels as though it is taking a deep breath in.

www.yvettemarks.co.uk